D1631588

A TUDOR KITCHEN

Peter Chrisp
Illustrations by Bill Donohoe

CONTENTS

**Produced for Heinemann Children's Reference by
Roger Coote Publishing, Gissing's Farm
Fressingfield, Suffolk IP21 5SH**

Educational Consultant: Jane Shuter
Editorial Director: David Riley
Art Director: Cathy Tincknell
Production Controller: Lorraine Stebbing

First published in Great Britain in 1997 by
Heinemann Children's Reference
an imprint of Heinemann Educational Publishers
Halley Court, Jordan Hill, Oxford OX2 8EJ
a division of Reed Educational & Professional Publishing Ltd

MADRID ATHENS PRAGUE FLORENCE PORTSMOUTH NH
CHICAGO SAO PAULO SINGAPORE TOKYO MEXICO
MELBOURNE AUCKLAND IBADAN GABORONE
JOHANNESBURG KAMPALA NAIROBI

ISBN 0431 06822 4 (Hbk) ISBN 0431 06823 2 (Pbk)

British Library Cataloguing in Publication Data
A catalogue record for this book is available from the British Library.

Printed and bound in Italy

THE GREAT HOUSE

This book is about a day in the life of a kitchen. The kitchen was in a 'great' (important) house, owned by a rich nobleman in the 1590s. The monarch at this time was Queen Elizabeth I, the last ruler from the family called the Tudors.

The nobleman owned a great deal of land. The grounds of his house included an orchard, for fruit; gardens, for vegetables and herbs; and a park, where herds of deer were kept for hunting. Beyond the grounds, there were several farms which he also owned. Some of these were run to supply food for the house – meat from herds of cattle and sheep; wheat and barley from the fields; and milk from the cows. Other farms were rented out to make money.

▲ Local farmers lived in small houses like this one. Unlike the great house, it had no glass in its windows.

▼ A 'great' house was built to look as impressive as possible, with many large windows. Glass was very expensive, and windows were a way of showing how rich you were.

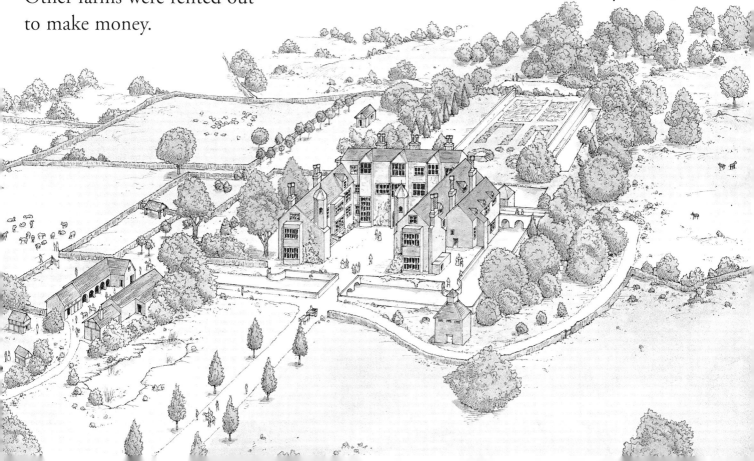

WORKERS IN THE KITCHEN

The most important servant in the great house was the steward. He ran the house and told all the other servants what to do. He kept the house's accounts, paid the servants' wages and ordered supplies of food from his master's farms. Other supplies, such as spices and sugar, he bought from the nearest town. The steward kept a close eye on the kitchen workers, making sure that they didn't steal or waste the food.

Men, women and children worked together in the kitchen of the great house. There were certain jobs, such as collecting eggs from the hen yard and making butter and cheese, which were always done by women.

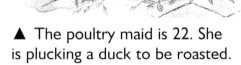

▲ The poultry maid is 22. She is plucking a duck to be roasted.

▲ A sixteenth-century kitchen maid shows off her well-stocked kitchen. She wears a leather apron, to wipe her greasy hands on.

◀ The cook, who is 52, checks to see if the boiled meat is ready.

4

► The chief male cook, who is 43, chops meat on his butcher's block, an old tree trunk. He needs a lot of strength, for butchering and skinning animals. Behind him, filling pies, is the pastry cook. She is 29.

Jobs that needed strength, such as butchering a pig, were often done by men.

In our Tudor kitchen, there were three main cooks. There was a male cook who was in charge of the roasting and boiling of meat. The female cook's speciality was making rich, spicy sauces to go with the meat.

A second woman, the pastry cook, made pies and baked bread in the oven. The poultry maid plucked and prepared birds for cooking. There was also an assistant male cook and a kitchen maid. They spent a lot of their time chopping and mixing ingredients.

The youngest workers in the kitchen were two small boys called the scullions. Their main job was sitting by the fire, turning meat as it roasted on a spit. They also had to sweep the kitchen and do the washing up.

► The assistant male cook is 29. He and one of the scullions are carrying food to the dining room. The other scullion helps the kitchen maid, who is 18. The scullions are aged 9 and 10.

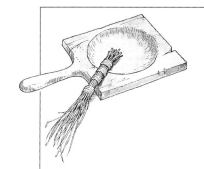

THE TUDOR KITCHEN

In the great house, the kitchen was just one of several rooms where meals were prepared. It was a large room where food was cooked over open fires. Its high ceiling helped reduce the smoke and heat. There wasn't much furniture in the kitchen – just two big tables used as work surfaces, and a couple of stools.

Along the corridor from the kitchen was another room for cooking. It was called the pastry, and was where bread and pies were baked in big ovens. Next to the pastry was the brewhouse, where the cooks made ale – from barley, yeast and water – and beer, which was ale with hops added. Butter and cheese were made in a room called the dairy.

▶ Here you can look down into the kitchen. The great roasting fire is at the top, while the stove is on the left. When they are ready, dishes are carried through the door on the left to be served in the hall or taken upstairs to the dining room. The two doors on the right lead to the brewhouse, the dry larder, the pastry and the scullery.

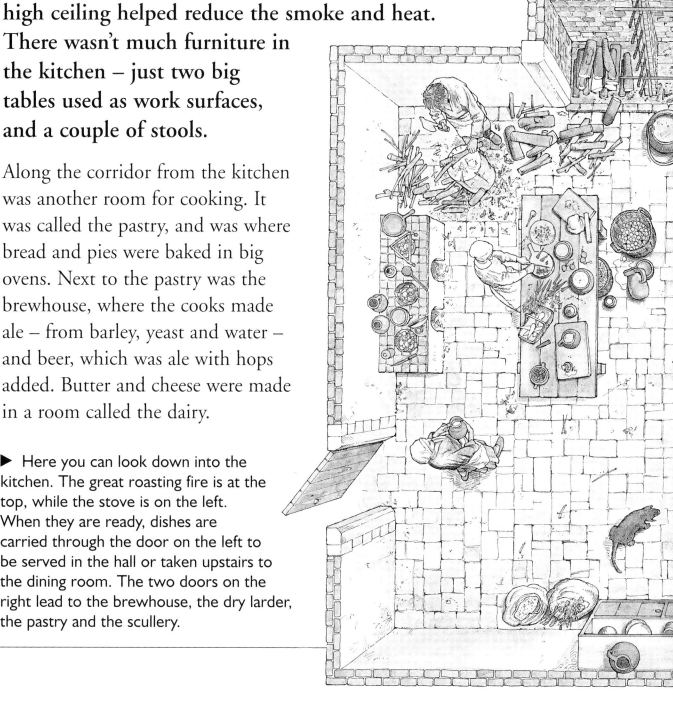

Food was not stored in the kitchen, because the fires made the room too hot. Fish, meat and butter would go off quickly if left in the kitchen. The house had several cool storerooms, called larders, where enough food was stored to stock a small modern supermarket. There was a wet larder for fish: both dried and pickled fish in barrels, and fresh fish, sometimes packed in seaweed.

▲ This plan shows part of the house, including the kitchen, the storerooms and the hall where feasts were held.

In the dry larder, there were tubs of flour, almonds and spices. The flesh larder was full of joints of meat, hanging from the ceiling on hooks.

Barrels of ale, wine and beer were kept in the buttery. Its name comes from the word 'butt', meaning barrel, and has nothing to do with butter. Bread was stored in the pantry. Finally, there was the scullery, where all the washing-up was done by the scullions.

COOKING METHODS

The most important part of the kitchen was the big arched fireplace. Joints of meat were roasted on spits, or boiled in metal cauldrons over a wood fire. To control the heat, the cauldron was raised or lowered above the flames, using a jagged piece of metal called a ratchet hanger.

▶ Part of the kitchen at Hampton Court, with two great fireplaces. The oven, in the right-hand fireplace, was added long after the Tudor period.

A roasting joint of meat had to be kept turning so that it cooked evenly and did not burn. This was usually done by hand. The scullion crouched on one side of the fire, slowly turning a handle attached to the spit. Another way was to use a dog wheel. Small dogs, specially bred for their short legs, ran round and round inside a wheel which turned the joint.

As well as the fireplace, the best Tudor kitchens had a stove, a brick bench with metal baskets. Charcoal was burned in the baskets, and cooking pots stood above the heat, resting on iron frames, or 'gridirons'. The stove was useful for frying and making sauces.

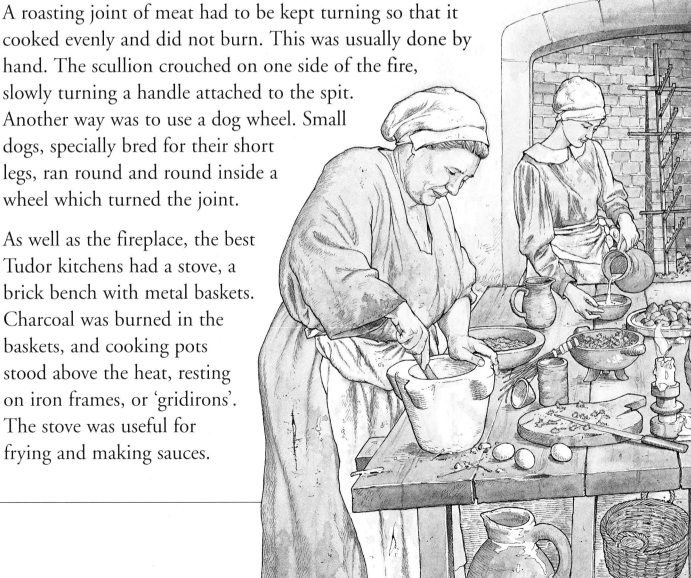

Pies and bread were baked in the big brick ovens in the pastry. A fire was lit inside using dried twigs, and this heated up the brick sides of the oven. Once the oven was hot enough, the burning twigs were swept out and the bread was pushed inside to be baked.

The cooks had many small kitchen tools. The most important were the pestle and mortar, for grinding and mixing; knives and cleavers for chopping; and peeled twigs tied into bunches for whisking.

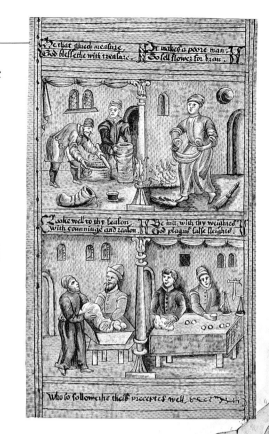

▶ These pictures from the 'Ordinances of the Bakers of York' show some of the stages in bread-making, including mixing and kneading the dough and weighing out loaves for baking.

◀ Everything had to be done by hand in the kitchen. While some of the workers chop, grind and mix ingredients, the scullion crouches by the fire, turning the roasting meat on its spit. He is protected from the heat by a disc of wet straw.

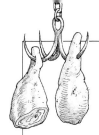

FOODSTUFFS

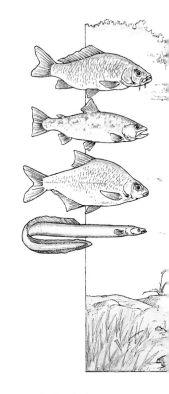

In Tudor times, rich people ate enormous amounts of meat and fish. They looked down on most vegetables as 'beggary baggage' – food fit only for the poor. They preferred meat to fish, but they were only allowed to eat meat on certain days, called 'flesh days'. Fridays, Saturdays and the 40 days before Easter were all 'fish days', when it was against the law to eat meat.

◀ A stag, killed during the hunt, is carried to the flesh larder.

Eating fish on special days had been a religious custom, imposed by the Catholic Church. By the 1590s England was no longer a Catholic country. However, Queen Elizabeth kept the custom going to encourage the fishing industry.

▲ Huntsmen set off with their pack of dogs, to kill some deer.

The great house had its own supply of meat. Apart from the farm animals, there was a deer park, with herds of deer. Rich men and women loved to hunt deer on horseback, following packs of hunting dogs. They also hunted boar (wild pigs) and wild birds using hawks. Birds were also trapped in nets by a servant called the birder. Every kind of bird was eaten, with larks and blackbirds as favourites.

For fish, the house had a pond stocked with carp and tench, and there were trout in the local river. The steward also bought barrels of pickled herring and dried salted cod, the two cheapest fish available. Dried cod was so hard that it had to be beaten with a hammer and then soaked before it could be eaten.

▲ Fishing in the pond of the great house. You can see four types of fish caught: (from the top) a carp, a trout, a bream and an eel.

Foods produced overseas included wine, spices, raisins, almonds and sugar. These foods were all very expensive. Rich people liked sugar so much that their teeth often rotted. Letters and diaries from the time tell us that foreign visitors were often shocked by the black teeth of wealthy English people.

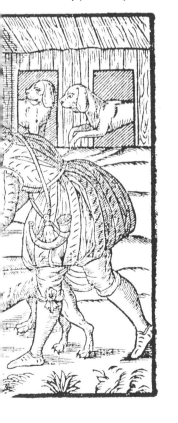

► The meat cook, helped by the scullions, is hanging up rabbits in the flesh larder.

SEASONAL FOODS

▼ A stag is skinned in the flesh larder. Rich Tudors liked venison more than any other meat, especially in pies.

Today, we can eat most foods all year round, thanks to fridges and fast transport. But in Tudor times, people ate the food that was grown at that time of year.

Most fresh fruit was eaten in the autumn, when the trees in the orchard produced their crop of apples, pears, plums and cherries. Some fruits, such as apples, could be stored to last the winter. Others had to be bottled in a syrup made from wine, sugar and spices.

Most farm animals were killed in the autumn, as there was never enough food to keep them all going through the winter. Only the strongest cows and sheep were kept alive for breeding the following year. So fresh beef and mutton were only available in summer and autumn. Pigs could be kept through the winter, because they ate leftover food and acorns.

▼ The gardener uses an axe to dig a small trench in the ground for planting vegetables.

Meat was preserved by rubbing it with salt. This drew out the moisture, the main cause of meat going rotten. The salted joints were then hung up in the larder. Salted meat had to be soaked in water to get rid of some of the saltiness. It was usually cooked with spices, especially pepper, to improve its flavour. In winter, the nobleman and his family ate large amounts of salted meat, but they had fresh meat, too, thanks to their deer parks. This food also varied from season to season. Does (female deer) were only hunted in the winter, when they were not nursing their young. Summer was the time to hunt bucks.

Another source of fresh meat was the dovecot, a brick building where pigeons were kept. Local farmers hated the pigeons because they ate the seed planted in winter. But the rich would not go without pigeon pie.

▶ Joints of meat are rubbed with salt, drying them out and making them last longer. This was a big job which had to be done every autumn.

MORNING IN THE KITCHEN

At sunrise, the kitchen workers were up, sweeping the floor and getting breakfast ready. This was a simple meal, which many people did not bother with at all. No cooking was involved. There was cold meat or fish, depending on whether it was a fish or a flesh day. This was served with bread baked the day before.

▼A Tudor brewhouse. Water was heated in the big vat on the left, and then poured into the tub on the right, where barley was stirred in. Hops and yeast were added, and in a few days the mixture fermented to become beer.

Several types of bread were eaten, made from wheat, rye or barley flour. The rich preferred manchet, fine white bread made with wheat flour. Bread was stored in a 'bread car', a big wooden tray hanging from the ceiling. The tray stopped rats and mice getting at the bread.

◀ Barrels of wine, ale and beer were stored in a room called the buttery, and the servant in charge was called the butler. Here the butler is filling jugs with ale for breakfast.

There was no tea or coffee, and water was seldom clean enough to drink. People drank ale, beer or wine. Even little children drank 'small beer', the weakest in alcohol. These drinks could be warmed, spiced, or sweetened with honey.

The servants carried the breakfast upstairs to the family, who ate in their rooms. Then the servants ate their breakfast of bread and ale. The hard work in the kitchen began at 10 am. The workers chopped wood and lit the fires in the hearth and in the baking ovens. The pastry cook mixed the dough for the day's bread baking, and rolled out pastry for the pies. The kitchen maid plucked birds of their feathers and chopped herbs for sauces. The meat cook brought in a side of pork and stuck it on a spit. It was time to start cooking the main meal of the day, dinner.

▲ The assistant cook and the scullion are chopping wood into small pieces called 'kindling', needed to get the fire going.

▶ While the scullions build a new fire, the pastry cook rolls out the dough for fish pies.

DINNERTIME

▼ This painting shows the kitchen of a poor family, with a great cauldron over a central fire. The couple in the background are making butter in a churn. The meal on the table is pottage, served in wooden bowls.

As dinnertime approached, the kitchen grew hotter and hotter, and the air filled with smoke and grease from the roasting meat. One of the scullions sat by the fire turning the joint, drinking mugs of ale to keep cool.

In the cauldron above the fire, a joint of salted beef was boiled. The only way to cook salted meat was to boil it, for it was much too dry to roast. It had to be soaked for several hours before boiling, to soften it and to get rid of as much salt as possible.

▶ This fifteenth-century painting shows servants carrying food to the dinner table from the kitchen serving hatch on the left.

At the stove, the cook made sauces, to give flavour to the boiled meat. This is a recipe for a sauce to be served with pork, from *A Proper New Book of Cookery*, published in 1575: *'Take half vinegar and half verjuice (crab apple juice), a handful of parsley and sage chopped very small, an apple chopped very small. Then take the gravy of the pig with sugar and pepper and boil together.'*

▼ The cook makes sauces, heating them over a charcoal fire on the stove. Can you see the rats? With so much food about, they could be a big problem in Tudor kitchens.

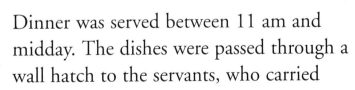

Dinner was served between 11 am and midday. The dishes were passed through a wall hatch to the servants, who carried them upstairs to the dining room. Several different meat dishes were served in the same meal. There might be pies stuffed with venison and blackbirds, roast and boiled pork, mutton and beef, as well as roast ducks and rabbits. People were not expected to eat everything. Instead, they chose a little from each of the dishes and sent the leftovers back down to the kitchen.

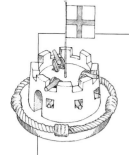

A TUDOR FEAST

On special occasions, such as a wedding, dinner became a feast. Instead of eating in the dining room, the family and their guests ate in the hall. Many more dishes were served than usual, and the cooks made sure that each one of them looked spectacular. The best silver plates and cups were brought out.

▲ Before every meal, people said 'grace', a short prayer thanking God for the food. Although this picture shows a Dutch family, a similar scene would have occurred at meal-times in Tudor houses in England.

A Tudor feast was made up of three courses. There were two meat courses, each with around a dozen different meat dishes. Then there was a third, sweet course, called the banquet. This was often served in a separate room or building, called the banqueting house. A banqueting house in the park was a nice place to eat in the summer.

Sweet dishes included preserved fruits, jellies, tarts and cakes. The most impressive-looking sweets were made from 'marchpane' (marzipan), a mixture of ground almonds, sugar and rose water. Marchpane was brightly coloured using vegetable dyes, such as saffron for yellow and parsley for green. It was then shaped into models of ships, castles, fruits, flowers and animals.

▲ A crowd has gathered for a great feast, held by the River Thames in 1600. Can you see four people carrying enormous pies?

▲ The servants bring out a boar's head and 'peacock royal', a bird which has been carefully skinned, cooked and then placed back inside its feathered skin. There are no forks on the table: everyone ate with their fingers or with spoons. People often used their own knives to cut the meat.

AFTERNOON IN THE KITCHEN

Once dinner had been served upstairs, the kitchen workers and other servants could eat their own meal. They sat around the kitchen table and said grace, a short prayer thanking God for their food. Only then could they eat.

The usual servants' dinner included pottage, a stew made with oatmeal or barley, herbs, and stock from the boiled meat. There were also leftovers from the dinner upstairs, such as half-eaten pies. Anything that the servants couldn't eat was given to beggars, who often waited at the gates of the house in the afternoons. Otherwise, leftovers were fed to the pigs and the hunting dogs.

▼ While the rich ate from pewter or silver dishes, their servants used wooden plates and bowls. The square wooden dish with a handle was called a 'trencher'.

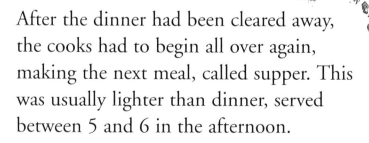

After the dinner had been cleared away, the cooks had to begin all over again, making the next meal, called supper. This was usually lighter than dinner, served between 5 and 6 in the afternoon.

◄ The Church taught that people should feed the hungry, clothe the naked and visit the sick – 'acts of mercy' shown in this painting. Beggars often arrived at the great house, hoping for leftovers from the feasts.

▶ These cooks are roasting different types of bird on spits. The cook on the left is pouring hot fat over the birds to stop them drying out as they cook.

On a fish day, a typical supper might include trout pasties. Thomas Dawson gave the recipe for these in his 1597 cookery book, *The Housewife's Jewel*. It shows that the Tudors loved sweet flavours, even with fish:

'Take a trout and seethe (boil) him. Then take out all the bones, then mince it fine with three or four dates... seasoning it with ginger and cinnamon, and a quantity of sugar and butter... Then take your fine pastry, and cut it in three corner ways (into triangles)... Lay your stuff in them, close them, and so bake them.'

THE END OF THE DAY

► The kitchen maid scrapes leftovers into a bucket for the pigs and the dogs.

After supper, the cooks could relax. They had their own light supper and went to bed as soon as it grew dark. It was left to the scullions and the kitchen maid to clear up the mess. They scraped the leftovers into a bucket, to be taken to the pigs, and went to the scullery to do the washing-up.

The scullions washed the dishes with water from the well in the yard. There was no washing-up liquid. They used sand for scrubbing pottery and wooden plates. Sand scratched metal dishes so the scullions scrubbed these with bundles of twigs and wiped them with cloths.

At last, their day's work was done. The scullions curled up under blankets on the kitchen floor. They fell asleep, warmed by the dying embers of the fire in the great hearth.

▼ One of the scullions washes and wipes the dishes.

THE TUDOR DIET

Meat provided three-quarters of the food of the rich. Although this sounds unhealthy, the meat was not as fatty as modern meat. Tudor farm animals were much less fat than modern beasts, and the deer and other game was also low in fat. A bigger problem was tooth-rotting sugar. Without vitamins from fresh foods, many people – rich and poor – suffered in winter from a disease called scurvy.

Poor people ate very different food from the rich. They had little meat and no sugar. In winter, they ate pottage made from dried peas and beans with a little bacon, if they were lucky. The 1590s was a bad time to be poor. There were five wet summers in a row, when heavy rains made the crops rot in the fields. Many poor people starved to death.

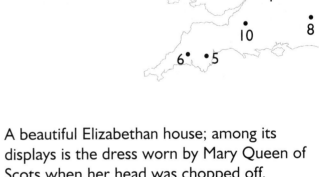

PLACES TO VISIT

Why not visit a great Tudor house and see for yourself what it was like to live in one? Some of the best are shown on this map.

1 Kentwell Hall, Long Melford, Suffolk (tel. 01787 310207). A large Tudor house; feasts and other Tudor events are held there.

2 Burghley House, Stamford, Lincolnshire (tel. 01780 52451). One of England's biggest Elizabethan houses, built in the 1580s.

3 Canon's Ashby House, Canon's Ashby, Daventry, Northamptonshire (tel. 01327 860044). A late Tudor manor house.

4 Charlecote Park, near Stratford on Avon, Warwickshire (tel. 01789 470277). Built in the 1550s, with its own deer park.

5 Compton Castle, Marldon, Paignton, Devon (tel. 01803 872112). Includes an early Tudor kitchen, dating from around 1520.

6 Cotehele Hall, St Dominick, near Saltash, Cornwall (tel. 01579 351346). Manor house with kitchen and dovecot.

7 Coughton Court, near Alcester, Warwickshire (tel. 01789 762435).

A beautiful Elizabethan house; among its displays is the dress worn by Mary Queen of Scots when her head was chopped off.

8 Hampton Court Palace, Kingston, Surrey (tel. 0181 781 9500). Includes the royal kitchens of Henry VIII, wonderfully restored.

9 Hardwick Hall, Chesterfield, Derbyshire (tel. 01246 850430). A late sixteenth-century house with orchards and herb garden.

10 Longleat House, Warminster, Wiltshire (tel. 01985 844400). A grand Elizabethan house with its own wildlife park.

11 Rufford Old Hall, near Ormskirk, Lancashire (tel. 01704 821254). A timber-framed Tudor hall.

INDEX

PICTURE ACKNOWLEDGEMENTS

Bridgeman Art Library 4 (Giraudon), 16 (Kunsthistorisches Museum, Vienna), 17 (British Library, London),
18 (Rafael Valls Gallery, London), 20 (Christies, London), 21 (Giraudon); ET Archive 10–11, 19; Historic
Royal Palaces 8; Image Select 9; National Trust Photographic Library 14 (Nick Meers); Topham 13. The map
on page 23 is by Peter Bull.